America,
A New Day Is Dawning

By Pastor Joyce Morris

LORD OF LIFE MINISTRIES
P.O. BOX 197
HAYMARKET, VA 20168

Radio Broadcast Schedule of Pastor Joyce Morris:

Albuquerque, NM	KXKS	10:00am-l0:15am	Sunday
Chattanooga, TN	WLMR	6:45am-7:00am	Sunday
York, PA	WYYE	7:00am-7:15am	Sunday
Greenville, SC	WELP	7:00am-7: 15am	Saturday
Asheville, NC	WSKY	12:30pm-12:45pm	Saturday
Omaha, NE	KLNG	10:15am-l0:30am	Saturday

TV Station Broadcast Schedule of Pastor Joyce Morris:

Prince William County • Comcast Channel 2
First two Sundays of every month at 6:30pm

Fairfax, VA • Cox TV Channel 10
Second Wednesday of every month at 7:00am
Second Thursday at 6:00pm and second Friday at 9:00am

ISBN 978-0615-40672-5

Published by Lord of Life Ministries
Joyce Morris
PO Box 197
Haymarket, Virginia 20168
www.lordoflifeministries.com

CONTENTS

INTRODUCTION

5

We wrote this book because so many people are confused in their minds as to what is going on in the world today. This book will give you the understanding of what is taking place all over the world and especially America. This book is about Christ being Lord of our lives. To declare the council of God to bring about the simplicity of Christ with balance. **Romans 5:17** This book is to teach, equip and encourage you to press ever deeper with your relationship with the Father. I dedicate this book to our Lord and Savior, and to the body of Christ. I pray that each person who reads this book will discover God's purpose for their lives.

Chapter 1
"THY GOD REIGNETH"

Some people have diligently sought the Father's understanding on what has been taking place in the world. He has answered different ones and shown them things by His Spirit, and by His word. However, the Father wants all of his people to understand and know what and why these things are coming to pass at this time. As you have noticed that things are escalating rapidly in this hour. God gave the World to man with a free will and man has done nothing but made a mess of things over a period of many years. Many times God gets the blame and people begin to get anger at God. When mankind has caused so many things in wrong decisions by being selfish, greed and evil.

We have been in the day of the Lord for some time now. Man's day is coming to an end with all the evil that is in the world. The Lord's judgments are present in the earth to bring forth his Kingdom, and to expose the corruption that is in the systems of the world.

Many people perish from lack of knowledge and understanding. This is why we want to share with you a number of visions that the father has given by his grace. They all tie in with what has taken place from 1993 and to this present time.

Isaiah 52:7 says, ***"How beautiful upon the mountains are the feet of him that bringeth good tidings, that publisheth peace; that bringeth good tidings of good, that publisheth salvation; that saith unto Zion, Thy God reigneth!"*** God wants His people to walk on top of the Mountain of the Lord, because as we do this (walk in the

Spirit), we can see that all things are working together for not only our good, but for the good of America and the entire world as well. He does not want us to walk in darkness, ignorance, or fear; He wants us to walk in the Light (understanding of God) and through the mind of Christ to see as He sees the end result of what He is doing. In Him we have already begun to see some of the good that has come out of the events that have happened. **Eph. 4:17-18**

As we stand in the Father and hold fast to the things He has shown us. Every time we go within to worship Him the Christ is going forth from within to publish Peace and bring Good tidings to His creation. By His Spirit we are declaring that our God reigns. No matter what is going on in your life and in the world around you, this alone should bring you Peace within, because thy God reigneth. The Lord wants me to share with His people as to what is really going on with the oil spill in the Gulf of Mexico. This is such good news and will give you such encouragement as to what God is saying about all of this.

I realize that many are being shaken by this and gripped with fear for their livelihoods and as to what the future holds. **Not long after the oil spill the Lord began to speak that this was His "SIGN". I asked the Lord what do mean that this is your SIGN. He answered and said, <u>"The earth shall be filled with the knowledge of the Glory of the Lord as the waters cover the sea. Hab. 2:14 and Isaiah 40:5 And the Glory of the Lord shall be REVEALED and all flesh shall see it together for the Lord hath spoken it.</u>**

The Lord began to explain as to what all this meant and said that this is getting ready to take place in His time. First He mentions about all the oil that was coming out of the earth into the sea and how man has been unable to stop the oil from coming out of the earth for such a long time. God is getting ready to show His power and glory through a people that will declare His Name throughout the earth. No man can stop what He is getting ready to do.

The word in **Isaiah 40:5** mentions *to be revealed –* **Revealed means: To be hidden for a certain time, to uncover, to be published, to show and to be put before the people.** All nations shall see this. Jesus was hidden for thirty years and when He came into maturity He was brought out into the open to display **His redemption, deliverance and salvation before mankind.** He was the complete expression of the Father and His Kingdom. Jesus was God in the flesh demonstrating God's power and anointing to mankind. The Lord heard the groaning of Israel and saw their sorrows and burdens under their task masters. In due process of time He brought Moses from the backside of the desert to use him to deliver His people. **He raised Moses up to show His power and declare his name through out all the earth. Ex 9:16**

Read Ex. 2:23 and Ex. 3:7-9 In Rom. 8:18-19 this is about to take place saints for the Glory of Our Heavenly Father which by we cry Abba Father. In VS *18 FOR I RECKON THAT THE SUFFERINGS OF THIS PRESENT TIME ARE NOT WORTHY TO BE COMPARED WITH THE GLORY THAT SHALL BE REVEALED IN US. VS.19 FOR THE EARNEST EXPECTION OF THE CREATION WAITETH FOR THE MANIFESTATION OF THE SONS OF GOD. PRAISE GOD SAINTS!!!!*

Chapter 2
"EMPTY THE GOLDEN OIL"

The Lord took me to *Zech. 4:6 It mentions about the two olive trees saying not by might, nor by power, but by My Spirit sayeth the Lord of Hosts.* It also mentions about the two olive branches. What does all this mean? First of all two speaks of a true witness. This is a people who have learned that it is not by their own strength and power to accomplish what God is doing. They know that it is walking in the Spirit through the mind of Christ and allowing the Father to work through them. For we live and move and have our being in Him.

I also want you to notice the branches are a people abiding in Christ and they are emptying the "Golden Oil" out of themselves. The Golden Oil is God's nature, power and anointing being emptied out to mankind to deliver God's people.

Go with me to **Rev. 11:1 and there was given me a reed like a rod, and the angel stood saying, rise and measure the temple of God, and the altar and them that worship in it.** We are the temple of God and He is measuring us by His word to bring us unto the measure of stature of the fullness of Christ. These are those who are abiding in Him and worshipping Him in spirit and truth. They are standing in the Holy Place. It says in **Matt. 24:14 That this gospel of the Kingdom shall be preached in ALL the world for a witness unto ALL nations; and then shall the end come. In verse 15 When ye therefore shall see the abomination of desolation spoken of by Daniel the prophet, stand in the Holy Place.** This is the Secret Place of the Most High.

Ps. 91:1-2 To stand in the Holy Place is to love God and abide in Christ.

Notice that the two witnesses received power to bring great judgments in the earth. Just like the time of Moses and Elijah. The only way the Father can deliver His people out of the world will be through His great judgments. He separated Israel unto Himself and <u>brought them out of Egypt</u>. **Isaiah 26:9 With my soul I have desired thee in the night; yea with my spirit within me will I seek thee early for when thy judgments are in the earth, the inhabitants will learn righteousness.** There are so many things that the Lord has prevented from taking place, because of those who have a heart for him he lets them know when something is getting ready to happen. He can use a people to allow Christ to intercede through them to prevent certain things from not taking place. **In Job 37: 11-14 It mentions that he scattered his bright cloud and it turns around by his Counsels, that they may do whatsoever he commanded them upon the face of the world in the earth. He causeth it to come, whether for CORRECTION, or for his land, or for MERCY. Harken unto this, O Job; stand still, and consider the wondrous works of God.** To give you an example : A terrorist tried to attack New York City with a bomb in a van that was never used. They also tried to assassinate President Bush and Prime Minister Tony Blair that same evening which was directed toward the White House. This all took place July the 4th, 2008. The Lord gave a vision in our meeting about this before it took place to have others interceding for God's will to be done not man's and to use our authority in Christ. Also at Thanksgiving in 2009 he warned us again that something was getting ready to take place at Christmas. This was the terrorist on the plane that had a bomb that didn't go off. It is important to stay in tune with the Lord and to listen to Him and allow Him to use you to bring about his purpose in the earth. The Lord has allowed certain things to happen in degrees, because he wants us to wake up and return back to him.

Chapter 3
"THE DAYS OF NOAH"

Matt. 24:37 The coming of the Lord will be even as the days of Noah. As you can see many people were cut off from the earth in Noah's time. There were the son's of God at that time that went into the daughters of men. Meaning they refused to walk with God and agree with His word. They became very carnal with every imagination and thought. Noah moved with fear and built the ark. He walked with God and obeyed Him. God told him when to bring his family and the animals into the ark before the flood. If you look at the scriptures very closely you will see, as the waters increased the ark went higher and it says that God shut him in. The Lord closed the door and shut the foolish out and shut Noah in the Ark.

Isaiah 26:20 Come, my people, enter thou into thy chambers, and shut thy doors about thee: hide thyself as it were for a little moment, until the indignation is overpast.
Isaiah 26:21 For, behold, the LORD cometh out of his place to punish the inhabitants of the earth for their iniquity: the earth also shall disclose her blood, and shall no more cover her slain.

Gen. 7:16-18 In verse 17 and the flood was forty days upon the earth, and the waters increased and bore up the ark, and it was lifted up above the earth. In verse 18 And the waters prevailed, and were increased greatly upon the earth, and the ark went upon the face of the waters. Notice it says that the waters prevailed exceedingly upon the earth and it covered the mountains, and all the flesh died.

The word prevailed means: to triumph, greater in strength, prevailed against greater odds, to persuade successfully.

God is not going to destroy the flesh this time with the water, but with His consuming fire, which are His great judgments on the earth.   Our heavenly Father will succeed in all that He has promised to do.

Waters represent your understanding, and the more truth the Lord reveals to you will cause your mountains to come down and you go higher in the realm of the Spirit. Mountains always represent a state of the mind. The more understanding you have in God's word and begin to apply it to your life; you begin to walk in the mind of Christ, which is the mountain of the Lord, Mt. Zion. This higher realm is beyond matter;   beyond soulish emotions and being controlled by your five senses. It is walking with your mind renewed by His word and obeying it. You will come into His complete rest in the Kingdom of God.

There are so many people that live in the sea and they are very restless in their soul.   Sea represents human thoughts that bring you out of your rest in God. **Isaiah 57:20 but the wicked are like the troubled sea when it can not rest, whose waters cast up mire and dirt.** Who are the wicked? They are those who refuse to submit to the Love of Christ and refuse to obey His word. **Hab.1:14 and makest men as the fish of the sea, as the creeping things that have no ruler over them**. This is truly the hour for us to allow the King of Kings, JESUS, to take His rightful place in us and be Lord of our life.

The ark ended up on Mt. Ararat in the seventh month on the seventeenth day of the month in a complete rest. **Mt. Ararat means: High land, higher realm; being in a** complete rest in God. **The number seven means complete and perfection**.

The oil that is lying upon the waters of the sea is a sign from God that **the earth shall be filled with the knowledge of the Glory of the Lord as the waters cover the sea. Hab.2:14 This gospel of the Kingdom shall be preached in all the nations for a Witness and then shall the End come. Matt. 24:14**

Ps. 107:25-30 Mentions that the Lord commandeth and raiseth up the stormy wind which lifteth up the waves and their soul melts, because of trouble. They are at their wits end. Then they cry unto the Lord in their trouble, and He bringeth them out of their distresses. I have had many storms in my life, but God has always been faithful to deliver me out of them all. Maybe you have a storm in your life and the Lord is trying to get your attention to turn to Him for help. He will hear your cry, as you cry out to Him, he will bring your soul into a rest.

God maketh the storm to calm so the waves are still. The Lord on High is mightier than the noise of many waters, than the waves of the sea. Notice how restless the sea is when you go to the beach and watch the waves come in. The waves represent our negative thoughts that take us out of God's peace and rest in our soul. In verse 30 it mentions: **then are they glad because they are quiet; so He bringeth them into <u>their desired haven</u>.** Jesus died so you can have peace in your mind and rest in your soul. God is greater than all the noise of your thoughts that are in your mind. **Peace be still and know that He is God.**

Start casting God's word upon the waters of your understanding and after many days it shall come to pass.

Cast thy Bread upon the Waters of your understanding for thou shall find it after many days. Ec. 11:1-2

Chapter 4
"THE SEA OF GLASS"

The Lord is casting His net into the sea (mankind), which is His message that is about the Kingdom of Heaven. Matt. 13:47-49 again the Kingdom of heaven is like a net that was cast into the sea and gathered every kind which when it was full, thy drew to shore; and sat down and gathered the good into vessels, but cast the bad away. So shall it be at the end of this age. The angels shall come forth and separate the wicked from the righteous, and shall cast them into the fire, There shall be wailing and gnashing of teeth.

In Rev. 15:1-3 It mentions about the last seven plagues. In verse 2 and I saw, as it were, a sea of glass mingled with fire, and them that had gotten the victory over the beast, and over his mark, and over the number of his name, standing on the sea of glass, having the harps of God. In verse 3 and they sing the song of Moses, and the song of the Lamb saying, Great and marvelous are Thy works, Lord God Almighty just and true are thy ways, thou King of saints.

The Lord wants me to break this down by His Holy Spirit. It is so simple. The simplicity of Christ is so wonderful. The number fifteen means: Rest; abiding in Christ. Here is a people that have come into a complete rest in Christ. Notice it is a sea of glass mingled with fire. They have been through the fire and have had their minds transformed into the mind of Christ. They have overcome the beast, that Adam nature, and the Spirit of Satan the antichrist, through Our Lord Jesus Christ. There is so much more we can say about this, but we must move along to the part of them singing the two songs. Also notice they are standing on top of the sea having the harps of God. They have learned how to live above their circumstances, trials and emotions through Christ and His word. The Bible says that He hath raised us up together, and made us to sit together in heavenly places in Christ Jesus NOW! **Eph. 2:6**

They sing the Song of Moses and the Song of the Lamb. The Lord heard the groaning of Israel and saw their bondages and sorrows. He also knows your bondage and sorrows which Christ died for us to be delivered of our bondages, and He bore our sorrows on the cross. God raised Moses up to deliver His people out of Egypt (world) with great judgments. *Ex. 9:16 For this cause I have raised thee up to SHOW in thee MY POWER; and that My Name may be declared throughout all the earth.* The overcomers are also singing the Song of the Lamb of His redemption and the New Covenant that He issued in on the cross. Praise God we will see such a great harvest come in all over the world and see the Majesty of God.

Chapter 5
"ARISE TO A HIGH PLACE"

Take a look at **Amp.** *Isaiah 60:1-7, Arise from depression and prostration in which circumstances have kept you-rise to a New Life! Shine be radiant with the Glory of the Lord, for your light has come, and the Glory of the Lord has risen upon you. In verse 5 Then you shall see and be radiant, and your heart shall thrill and tremble with joy (at the glorious deliverance and be enlarged, because the abundant wealth of the sea shall be turned to you, unto you shall the nations come with their treasures. Also in Psalm 91:1-14.*

The only way you will ever arise is to have your mind renewed by God's word and change the way you think. If not we will remain the same and never come into all that God has promised us for His glory. Truly it is by His grace, mercy and truth that gets us there. We must be willing to change and obey His word. **Keep thy heart with all diligence, for out of it are the issues of life.** Notice it says, *out of the heart are the issues of life.* Not upon the heart are the issues of life, <u>but out of the heart</u> are the issues of life. WOW! Read **Prov. 4:20-24**. This means that a lot more of our issues are happening, because of the way we think. It does not mean all of your issues, because there are other people that persecute you that are in the world and hate the Christ in you. I believe in a balance in God's word.

The Lord spoke to me to re-read **Isaiah 60:7** again, and He asked me this question, do you know who Kadar is and his brother, Nebaioth? I really had never looked into this, but I got so excited when I found out and saw that they gathered all their flocks, and shall come up with acceptance of the Lord's altar. They are the two sons of Ishmael. Praise God they will accept the altar of Christ. Not all will come, but many will come into the Kingdom of God.

Chapter 6
"THE VALLEY OF DECISION"

I believe there are people out there today all over the world who are in the valley of decision. To those in the valley of decision, God is saying, "Are you ready? I am waiting for you to yield to Me. I am waiting to be supreme in your life. I am waiting to be Lord over you. Are you tired of being in control? Are you tired of ruling this house, ruling this temple? Will you make the decision today to come to Me and allow Me to take over your life completely? Will you let go of these things that you are holding on to?" Many people all over the world are in the valley of decision. The good news is that the only thing that brings them in is the fire of the Lord. The heat has been turned up in the world. Through the heat and what the Father is allowing to take place in the world, the greatest harvest that mankind has ever known or seen, will take place. I am excited about what is coming. Every Christian I talk with has a knowing within that things are very close for the coming of the Son of Man, Our Lord Jesus Christ. They know that there is something ready to explode, something ready to take place.

Chapter 7
"THE GRAND FINALE"

The Lord told me that He has His own stage. He has already put His sons on the stage, and the curtains are ready to be pulled open for the WHOLE world to see God's GRAND FINALE. The world will see the glory of the Lord, the manifestation of Christ. God will demonstrate His power for His Glory through His sons. There is a joy that the Father has. There is also a sadness that the Father has for those who will not yield to His Lordship. The Lord is grieved that He will have to cut them off from the earth. He grieves over it, but He will lose nothing. You will have to get my book, The Book of Life, to understand that His love will never fail. Those who would not yield could have had the opportunity of living in harmony in His kingdom through the millennial age.

Another scripture I wanted to show you is *Psalm 98:1-4,* *"O sing unto the Lord a new song; for He hath done marvelous things: his right hand, and his holy arm, hath gotten Him the victory." 2 The Lord hath made known his salvation: his righteousness hath He openly shewed in the sight of the heathen."* In the sight of all the nations in Moses' time it was shown. In the sight of all the nations in the time of Jesus it was shown. In the sight of all the nations once again it will be shown—His salvation and His kingdom. It says, His kingdom will be preached to all nations for a witness. It didn't say they would believe it, but it will be a witness. Then the end shall come. We read again in *Verse 3,* which says, he *hath remembered his mercy and his truth toward the house of Israel.* "America became

spiritual Israel when Israel rejected the Kingdom of God. This will be explained to you more later in the book. The Lord is going to set the United States of America free. She is going to be in humility, serving the one true living God and being the spiritual Israel that God has called her to be. *Verse 3* continues, *"All the ends of the earth have seen the salvation of our God." Verse 4 "Make a joyful noise unto the Lord, all the earth: make a loud noise, and rejoice, and sing praise."* This is the good news. Matt 21: 35-44 verse 43 Therefore I say unto you, The kingdom of God shall be taken from you (natural Israel) and given to a nation bringing forth the fruits of it. Romans 11:15-26 For if the casting away of them be the reconciling of the world, what shall the receiving of them be, but life from the dead. Verse 23 For God is able to graft them in again. Verse 20 And so all Israel shall be saved, it is written, there shall come out of Zion the Deliverer and shall turn away ungodliness from Jacob. God is able to graft natural Israel back in again, praise His wonderful Name! More of this is explained to you in Chapter 11.

Chapter 8
"FIRST LOVE"

Several years ago I had a vision of a bride. She had a wedding dress with a long train attached to it. Upon this train were all kinds of worldly goods. We asked the Father what does this mean? He said that this bride was representative of every human being in the world, that they have forgotten their **First Love** with Christ, and are caught up in the material/temporal things of this world rather than Him. They do not worship Him in Spirit and in Truth. They love the world more than Him, and have chosen to have a union with everything but Him. He said He would begin to **JUDGE** the economic system all over the world. He would do it in degrees and began with Japan. Like-minded countries, including the United States, believe that they have succeeded on their own. The Lord is humbling people all over the world because everything that is high and lofty against God will be made low and must come down. It will be by the grace of God and His love. He has to correct many things in order to issue in the new world, which is His Kingdom. To be brought down to humility is a good thing, because the humble shall hear and be glad. **Isaiah 2:11-12**

Isaiah 52:1 says, _Awake, awake, put on your strength O Zion, put on your beautiful garments, O Jerusalem the holy city._ He is telling us to shake off the dust, from walking in the carnal nature (fleshly desires) that our soul lusts after and causes us to be driven to go after worldly things and not after God. The Lord has a purpose in everything that he allows. He judged Japan by an earthquake. He caused a bank in England to collapse which caused Japan to lose many millions in stock. Money is not the problem - it is the love of it. When these things take God's place that is when we are out of balance and have lost our first love with Him. **ITim. 6:10**

Chapter 9
"PASS OVER AMERICA SEVEN TIMES"

In the end of 1992, New Years Eve, God gave me another vision. We saw many months and years flying by, rapidly. During those months and years, darkness increased in the earth. I saw floods, earthquakes and various disasters beginning to happen. Many people were waking up and coming to know God as their Savior, as their deliverer and their refuge. Sometimes it takes disasters to humble people so that they can receive the goodness of the Lord and all that he desires to give them.

The Lord spoke and said He would pass over America seven times, like He did Nebuchadnezzar in **Daniel 4:25-32,34,36**. He said that America had left her first love and America was in pride, greed and self-centeredness. The number seven means complete and perfection. **In Daniel 4:25 and seven times shall pass over thee, till thou know that the Most High ruleth in the Kingdom of men and giveth it to whomsoever He will. In verse 26 after thou shall know that the heavens do rule. Those who walk in pride He is able to abase.**

I will judge her like I did in the time of Moses." Egypt represents the world. God judges the very thing that man loves; the very thing that man worships and puts before God. He judged Egypt in degrees and then the judging increased as time went on. He said this would happen to America. The majority of Americans have not been awakened to realize what has been going on.

The attacks of September 11th have gotten the attention of the whole world. There is good news of what came out of this and what will continue to result from it. This is all part of God's plan. Remember God hardened Pharaoh's heart. Pharaoh was the enemy of Israel and he represented Egypt and everything that was against the Christ. We know that there are anti-Christ spirits in the world. God did say that man's heart would wax cold. Look at **Matthew 24:12, _There would be murder in men's hearts and they would not care or have feelings for another persons life_**. God had to use Pharaoh. He used the enemy to push Israel out of worldliness to bring a people into a place in Him where they would rely upon God, know Him as their Lord, and love Him as EL SHADDAI, the all-sufficient one. He wanted them to know that he would supply all their needs.

Pharaoh disobeyed, but God still used him to push Israel out of Egypt. God is using these terrible attacks to awaken America to bring her to her knees and to humble her. He is trying to bring America to a spiritual awareness. This is the good news of our Lord and Savior. He loves us enough to bring us to correction. We did lose many lives; many loved ones, we could have lost many more if it had not been for God's grace and kindness and mercy. The people who died did not die in vain. They had a cause in God's plan and he ministered to them on the other side.

Chapter 10
"AMERICA REPENT "

A woman had a vision of many who died in the attacks and saw that God received them so that they could go into Him. God does not lose anyone. God has been trying for years to wake America up and to get her out of her prejudice, her pride and her greediness. He wants her to understand that in the Kingdom of 'God there is righteousness, peace and joy. In God's Kingdom there is neither Jew nor Greek, there is neither bond or free, there is neither male nor female, for ye are one in Christ. We are all a part of each other. People all over the world are a part of one another. It has nothing to do with color or race. We all came out of God and all will be reconciled back into God. Amp. **Rom. 11:36 For from Him and through Him and to Him are all things. For all things originate with Him and come from Him; all things live through Him and all things center in and tend to consummate and to live in Him. To Him be the Glory Forever! Amen.** So Be It. As you read on you shall find more scriptures about this.

We have to begin to be kind to one another and show love toward one another. This terrorist attack caused America to forget about herself and not be caught up in self-centeredness. God moved in New York and people began to care about one another, hugging and helping each other. Unfortunately, it is a shame that it takes something like this to wake us up to what God has been saying all along. He has said that we must love one another and be kind to one another. Look at: *John 15:12, "This is My commandment, that you love one another, as I have loved you"* We must turn back to our first love with our heavenly Father for that is the most important thing in our lives. God has given us years of plenty, but now we need to learn how to depend on God. What is the whole purpose in these recent happenings? The good news is that God is in control, and He does reign. We are not to be caught up in fear. Look at **Proverbs 29,** ***The fear of man brings a snare but whoever puts his trust in the Lord; shall be safe.*** This is a time to rejoice.

Chapter 11
"SPIRITUAL ISRAEL"

It is true we do mourn and grieve for our country, but it is not a time for us to hate. God is love and merciful and just. It is a time for God's people to pray for the United States of America and for us to be guided by His wisdom and mercy. We must pray that He will bring about His correction in love and compassion. Even though He used Pharaoh to push Israel out of Egypt, God corrected Pharaoh at the Red Sea. The Father has a purpose for everything. He is a merciful God. We must be a people with forgiveness and mercy for others. We have been a country that has blessed our enemies. America has operated in the principles of the Kingdom of God many times. We have blessed and given to all of our enemies. This has been the plan of God, because America is spiritual Israel. God spoke in ***Mathew 21:42-43,*** ***"I have sent my servants and you killed them. I have sent my prophets and you have killed them. I will send my Son and you will kill Him. So to whom will I give the Kingdom of God? You have rejected the builder. You have rejected the stone, therefore I will give the Kingdom to another nation"*** The United States of America is the nation to whom God gave the gospel of the Kingdom of our Lord and Savior. We are to be a spiritual people and turn back to our first love in Christ. To be a beacon light to the nations that allows God to express and establish His Kingdom in them. To allow the Father to express His love and show just what His Kingdom is all about. Our Pledge states – One nation under God, with liberty and justice (freedom) for all. Our Father will fulfill that. He will bring it to pass, because the Kingdom of God must be preached to all nations as a witness and then shall the end come. His Kingdom is forever and it will not be moved. Therefore you need to come out of the world and enter into the Kingdom of God. **To be in the world but not of the world. Rom. 12:1,2**

Chapter 12
"AN ENDLESS SUPPLY"

In His kingdom, there is an endless supply, you will lack in nothing. Those of you who have lost your jobs – read *Matthew 6:33 <u>"Seek ye first the Kingdom of God and His righteousness and all else will be added unto you."</u>* As you put God first and have a love affair with Him, He will meet your needs. The Bible says the righteous shall not beg for bread. Therefore you need to know that God will take care of you even as He takes care of the lilies of the field and the birds of the air. He wants us to rely and depend on Him. This is the hour that Americans must return to putting God first in their lives. He wants us to put our trust wholly in Him and not try to do things in our own strength.

The Father gave a vision of something we thought would happen in the year 2000. We put the vision on a tape and sent it out, because we thought it was going to happen at that time. The vision was of a man being caught up to a high realm in God. This man was corporate. It was God's people who were all walking in the spirit and being more aware of God than ever before. They were walking in peace, joy and love in Christ. They were not walking in the flesh or in their emotions. God has tried, proven and tested a people. They have come to realize that God is in control and that all things work together for good for those who love Him. Therefore these are a people who can stand in the evil day and having done all, stand. They are not moved by what is happening in the world. They will stand firm and trust in the Lord and they will be like Paul. They will rejoice and be of good cheer. **Eph 6:13-14**

In **Acts 27:18-21,** Storms were hitting while Paul was in the ship. A storm causes us to cast off the weights. In the ship they laid aside their weights because of the storm. It seems that we do not want to look at things or get rid of anything until some problem comes along. Thank God that He loves us enough to allow these things to happen to make us look at things that He wants to change in our lives.

In the same vision there was a man holding a newspaper and he was trembling because of what he was reading. The Lord put a burden on some people at that time to be praying. I believe that whatever was going to happen was put off because God prevented it from happening at that time. Some men crossed the line into Canada, but they were caught. By the grace of God they were stopped, it was not God's timing. He had a plan and a specific day for it to happen. Later we will elaborate on why the attacks on New York had to happen on the eleventh day and why it was flight eleven. God does not miss anything. Everything goes exactly according to His purpose and His will. He is pointing out something for us to see. The Twin Towers in New York were a witness to the entire world. What was God trying to show us?

Chapter 13
"THE BABYLON SYSTEM"

I want to share something with you about Babylon. God has been telling His people to get out of Babylon for a very long time. Babylon is mans system. It is what man teaches and it has nothing to do with the Kingdom of God or the love of God. Babylon is a mixture and is the tree of knowledge of good and evil. It is man trying to do everything in his own strength. Babylon represents the things that we love more than God and the systems of the world. It is a representation of being confused in your mind. What are the gods or idols that we think about more than we think about God? They are what we constantly have on our minds, and the things for which we work and labor for. They all cause us to lose sight of God and His will and purpose. We are called for His will and purpose and not our own.

God has a plan for His Sons. He has been telling us to mature, and grow up and come out of the world. He has been gathering His Sons from the four corners of the earth to take their positions in Christ, to rule and reign with Christ now. It is **NOW !**

It has never been later. God has always wanted us to **RULE AND REIGN NOW**. He has need of you in this hour. He needs you to get in the spirit and to allow the mind of Christ to operate through you in order to minister all over the world by His spirit. ___"It is not by might, nor by power, but by my spirit,"___ saith the Lord. God can use you right in your home as you allow His thoughts to go out to creation. ___"Stretch forth your hands and heal the nations."___ This is what God wants His Sons to do. He is raising up His Sons to execute a word in this hour. A word, which the whole world is waiting to hear. He has to humble His people. They are not going to hear what He has to say until they are humbled. His word says, ___"The humble shall hear and be glad."___

Some of you have been waiting a long time to share what God has taught you, but God has kept you on the back burner. He has been burning out of you everything that is not like Him. He has set you there for a purpose and for this hour to share the gospel of the Kingdom of God. Not just to share but to express the Kingdom of God. Let your life be a witness to those around you. Let others see your peace, your stability and your trust in the heavenly Father.

The good news is that God has been judging Babylon for several years. It has been little by little and bit by bit. He judged England and her government. He spoke to us even before that judging and let us know that He was going to bring out the dirty laundry for the whole world to see. He was going to cause man to see the corruption in the government. Only the Kingdom of God is going to work. Man's ideas will not work forever. God's Kingdom will go on throughout eternity. His government will remain forever. God spoke after the judgment of England and said, "He would judge our country". That He would start at the top and go through Congress and all down the line. What is in our government is also in the people. There is adultery, fornication and immorality. We were pointing the finger at one man and we needed to take a good look at ourselves.

Chapter 14
"WAKE UP AMERICA"

God wants America to wake up, and come out of her slumber. This in not only about terrorists, but also about repentance. It is time for America to repent and for each individual to allow Christ to shine His light upon you. You cannot change yourself, but God can change you. God wants us to allow Him to uncover those things that are not like Him. Some of us have waited for a long time for something to happen to awaken us. This is part of Babylon coming down. Read ***Revelations 18.*** This chapter has some connection with what happened on September 11th. God spoke and said, " that this will not go according to man's plan, but it will go according to His plan." Babylon represents the world and the Lord is saying, ***"Come out of her and be ye separate." Read II Corinthians 6:14, "What does righteousness have to do with unrighteousness, what does light have to do with darkness? What have you got in common with Baal or with idols? Be ye separate and come out of her and He will be God in us."*** He will walk in us and talk through us and express who He is through us. He is saying come out of her My people. He is bringing plagues upon the earth. Haven't you noticed what has been going on? Many things have been happening with the birds, bees and mosquitoes – wake up> Look at ***Revelations 18:4, "I heard a voice from heaven saying, come out of her My people, that ye be not partakers of her sins and that ye receive not her plagues."*** This is the day for you to come in the ark, to abide in Christ, and to stand in the holy place. It is a time to put on the whole armor of God and stand in the evil day and having done all, stand. In *Revelations 18:5,* <u>*"Her sins have reached unto heaven and God hath remembered her iniquities." Verse 7, "How much she hath glorified herself, and lived deliciously, so much torment and sorrow give her for she saith in her heart, I sit a queen, and am no widow and shall see no sorrow."*</u>

America has been in a slumber, thinking that we would never have anything like September 11th. In *Revelation 18:9,* <u>*"The kings of the earth who have committed fornication and lived deliciously* **"kings are those who have authority and or rulers in the world"** *with her, shall bewail her and lament for her when they shall see the smoke of her burning." Verse 10, "standing afar off for the fear of her torment, saying Alas, Alas the great city Babylon that mighty city, for in one hour is thy judgment come." Verse 11,"and the merchants of the earth shall weep and mourn over her, for no man buyeth their merchandise anymore."*</u> God is creating a new heaven and a new earth; a new day is dawning. A new world is being issued in and that is the Kingdom of God. See *Revelations 18:14,* <u>*"and the fruits that thy soul lusted after are departed from thee, and all things which were goodly are departed from thee and thou shall find them no more." Verse 15, "The merchants of these things which were made rich by her, shall stand afar off for the fear of her torment, weeping and wailing."In Verse 16,"and saying alas, alas that great city that was clothed in fine linen and purple and scarlet, and decked with gold and precious stones and pearls." Verse 17, "for in one hour so great riches have come to naught and every shipmaster and all the company in ships, and sailors and as many trade by sea, stand afar off" Verse 18,"and cried when they saw the smoke of her burning, saying what city is like unto this*</u>

<u>great city."</u> ***When the Lord took me to verse 18. I knew it was the Twin Towers in New York City. I just about fell off my chair and said Lord have mercy on us all.***

When the terrorist attack happened in New York, everybody forgot about material things. They were just thinking about their loved ones. I met a woman who was in one of those buildings that collapsed. She was in the bathroom and when she came out there was no one there. She said it frightened her. Everyone had run out. She heard the voice of the Lord. He spoke to her and said leave now. She thought about her purse and the $600.00 with her driver's license. Again the Lord said, "Leave NOW and told her to let it go." She <u>obeyed</u> and her life was saved. The compassion of America came forth. There is such goodness in God's people. There is goodness in America and we must focus on that goodness that is in each other. We must learn that there is no color, no race, no Jew or Gentile in the Kingdom of God. We need to love one another for all of this is for God's purpose and for His glory. God knows exactly what He is doing. I was twenty miles from the Pentagon, and my house shook when the attack and explosion occurred. I was talking on the phone with my son, because we each saw the New York attack on TV. I had said "it will hit here in Washington DC also." We had no more spoken those words, when there was an explosion at the Pentagon.

God is shaking everything that can be shaken. He is shaking the heavens and the earth. That is in ***Hebrews 12:26,*** ***<u>"He is shaking everything that is not like His Kingdom and does not represent His Kingdom."</u>*** When God is finished the only thing that will remain is His Kingdom and it can not be moved. This is why you need to have the Kingdom of God established in you. In *Revelations 19: 1-3,* <u>*"I heard a great voice in heaven saying Alleluia: Salvation and glory, and honor and power unto the Lord our God. Verse 2, "for true and righteous are His judgments for He hath judged the great whore, which did corrupt the earth with her fornication and hath avenged the blood of His servants at her hand" Verse 3, and again they said, Alleluia and her smoke rose up forever and ever"*</u> The Father is telling us that this is a time of rejoicing, a time of worship and praise.

In <u>*Luke 21:25,*</u> Here the Lord said there would be signs in the heavens, moon, stars and the sun. We have shared with you why there is a hole in the ozone. It is a sign for the whole world to see. It is God's billboard sign. A sign that all that He has spoken is coming to pass. In *Luke 21:25,* <u>*"There shall be signs in the sun and in the moon and in the stars and upon the earth distress of nations, with perplexity; the sea and the waves roaring."*</u> The sea is humanity and the thoughts are roaring in their minds, full of fear and worry – wondering what their future holds. We know that God holds the future and that He wants us to live in the moment. We know that we are eternal people and that we will live throughout eternity. We know that death is just the beginning. The only thing that we lose is our body, but our life is throughout eternity. Yes there is a lake of fire, and yes the lake of fire is for purification. **Rev. 21:7:8** It is to purify those things in people that are not like God. Christ is that consuming fire. Therefore we know that Jesus can go on the other side with the keys of death and hell and reconcile them at a later time. Rev 1: 17-18. There is an order and timing for every individual. *1Cor 15:7* There is a time for each person to wake up. One morning at about 6 o'clock, I took a walk. God was showing me that not everyone wakes up at the same time. In the natural some wake up a 5:00am, some at 6:00am, and maybe some at noon. Some even sleep all day and do not wake up until nighttime. Spiritually God has an order for every individual to awaken in their time. In **Amp. ICor. 15:23-28** Notice it says **in His own order.** This is where the free will comes in. In verse 28, God will be in the end **all and in all. Read Phil. 2:10-11 That is why hell, The Lake of Fire, is on the other side. If you want to understand more about Heaven and Hell read my 2nd book, "The Book of Life". You will find that God has written a script for you in the Book of Life. Ps. 22:27-29, Is. 24:21-22, Is. 58:12-13, Phil 2;10-11, Rom 5:10-12,17-21, Rom 11:13-15,26-32, Col 1:20-23, 1 Cor 15:23,28.**

Chapter 15
"LIFT UP YOUR HEADS"

In *Luke 21:26,* <u>**"Men's *hearts failing them for fear and looking after those things which are coming on the earth; for the power of heaven shall be shaken."***</u> God does not want you to be caught up watching the news to the point that fear grips you. This is a time for you to be praying. Praying for our government leaders for God to guide and lead them. Pray that God will continue to enable us to come forth and be what He wants us to be. Lift up your heads and rejoice, because this is the day that the Lord has truly made and we will rejoice and be glad in it. What does that mean? Lift up your heads. Keep your mind on the Lord with praise and thanksgiving. Know that God is working to our good and that He is in control. It is His plan, and purpose, which is causing Babylon to come down so that man can receive the Kingdom of God. Truly the only way that we have received the Lord has been by being broken and humbled. The Lord will continue to humble man because He desires man to receive Him in all of His glory. It grieves God to bring about these things but necessary in order to bring about His plan and purpose.

God has been mentioned more than ever and many people are coming to the Lord. ***Philippians 2:10-11,*** <u>***"Every knee shall bow and every tongue shall confess that Jesus Christ is Lord to the glory of the Father."***</u> This is truly a day of repentance for every individual to have a change of mind and return to their first love with Christ. Do not be encumbered about with the cares of this world. Take time to develop your relationship with the Lord. No one can do it for you. Are you strong in Him? Are you deeply rooted in the word of God? Deeply rooted in Christ and the Word so that you will be able to stand and having done all, to stand in the evil day. Walk by faith and not by sight. The Lord will cause us to come up higher in Him as we walk in the spirit each day. We will keep that peace in our minds. We will not be caught up in fear and worry but will learn to trust Him moment-by-moment and day-by-day. Depend on God the way a little child depends on his mother and father. God wants us to humble ourselves and depend on Him and receive Him. He wants a love affair with each one of us. God loves us so much. He wants each of us to be established in Him so that we will not be moved in this day and this hour as He continues to do His work. You will see His power and glory as never before, because He will declare who He is in all His glory. He is the Lord; the Almighty God. A true and living God and a loving merciful Father. Thank God, that He knows what He is doing. It is by His grace that we have gotten where we are in Him. We love and appreciate each and every one of you. This is the day of rejoicing because we are going to be able to share with others in a way that we never have before. People will be willing to hear what God has to say when they are broken and humbled. So rejoice and keep your eyes upon Him.

Chapter 16
"THE WAR IN IRAQ"

Another thing I want to share with you is about the war. There is so much misunderstanding about the war. Over the years I have learned to seek God for the answers, because He is always right. What God is saying is always the opposite to what man is saying.

Two months before the war the Lord gave a very important vision that I will never forget. In this vision there was a woman standing in the desert all bent over and crying out, "when is God going to help us." It reminded me of the scripture in **Luke 13:10-14** All of a sudden I saw Jesus standing in front of the woman. I asked the Lord, who is this woman and He said it was the Iraqi people and that He had heard their cry. He said that Sadam was a beast and had ruled over the people long enough and He was going to bring his regime down and he would be hung just like Haman in the Book of Esther.

God spoke again and said that America was the only country that He could use and that He would put His love in the American soldier's hearts and many would be willing to die for her. He spoke again and said that He would raise up a man to stand with President Bush and that two is a true witness. It ended up being Prime Minister Tony Blair in England. I am not a Republican or a Democrat. I believe in seeking God as to who He wants us to vote into office. In the vision the last thing that I saw was the woman slowly coming up little by little. So I knew the war would be long. In fact it has been a very slow process.

I asked the Lord why are you so interested in this country? Other countries have similar issues and weapons and hate America just like Iraq. He revealed that Iraq was the cradle of man; **the Garden of Eden**, where everything started in the beginning. He spoke that He must start in Iraq to bring down the task master. There is so much anger and misunderstanding over the war. God has the answers for everything. If only we would spend more time with Him for the answers and ask Him and not lean on our own understanding or man's opinion.

God spoke again after the vision and mentioned that many countries would turn against us for fear that we would bring change in their countries to liberate the people. All this has taken place as to other countries hating us. America has blessed her enemies many times. The week before the terrorist attacks on September 11th, the Father gave a word on being caught up in God. Then the Friday night before the attacks, He gave a vision of many dark clouds coming. In the Spirit we saw hundreds of people running in fear because they did not understand what was happening. Then the Lord spoke and said, **"Be not afraid. Stand firm, and hold fast to the Word that He has given to us. Your stability and Peace is only found in Me. Lean not upon your own understanding, for I will explain to you what is going on. Good shall come out of this. It shall be for My purpose and My Glory."**

Many people believed that the government will save us, and bring us out of this mess that we are in. The only thing that will save America is when she has **REPENTED. 2 Chron 7:14. If my people who are called by name, shall humble themselves and pray, and seek my face, and turn from their** wicked ways, then will I hear from Heaven, and will forgive their sin, and will heal their land. Amen.

We have lots of material on each subject that was covered in this book and were unable to put it in at this time. We have many newsletters, CDs and DVDs on the Website that you can get more information on everything that we shared with you in this book. www.lordoflifeministries.com For example we have news letters about Babylon coming down , The Four World Empires, Restoring Generations, Salt 1, Salt 2, The New World Coming and many other materials that will help you. We pray that you will seek God to show you personally these truths, and to grow deeper in the Lord through his love and grace. May God continue to bring America back to her first love with Him. God Bless America Amen!

9 780615 406725